Contractions
at the Zoo

By Kathleen Connors

Gareth Stevens
Publishing

Please visit our website, www.garethstevens.com. For a free color catalog of all our high-quality books, call toll free 1-800-542-2595 or fax 1-877-542-2596.

Library of Congress Cataloging-in-Publication Data

Connors, Kathleen.
Contractions at the zoo / Kathleen Connors, Gareth Stevens.
    p. cm. — (Word Play)
Includes index.
ISBN 978-1-4339-7184-6 (pbk.)
ISBN 978-1-4339-7185-3 (6-pack)
ISBN 978-1-4339-7183-9 (library binding)
1. English language—Contraction—Juvenile literature. 2. Contraction—Juvenile literature. 3. Language arts (Primary) I. Stevens, Gareth. II. Title.
PE1161.C66 2012
421'.54—dc23
                                        2011050606

First Edition

Published in 2013 by
Gareth Stevens Publishing
111 East 14th Street, Suite 349
New York, NY 10003

Copyright © 2013 Gareth Stevens Publishing

Designer: Andrea Davison-Bartolotta
Editor: Kristen Rajczak

Photo credits: Cover, pp. 1, 19 iStockphoto/Thinkstock; cover, p. 1 (sign) Pablo H. Caridad/ Shutterstock.com; p. 5 Dmitriy Shironosov/Shutterstock.com; p. 7 Colman Lemar Gerardo/ Shutterstock.com; p. 9 E. O./Shutterstock.com; p. 11 Anan Kaewkhammul/Shutterstock.com; p. 13 Jay Si/Shutterstock.com; p. 15 Muellek Josef/Shutterstock.com; p. 17 Fuse/Getty Images; p. 20 Igor Kovalchuk/Shutterstock.com.

Printed in the United States of America

CPSIA compliance information: Batch #CS12GS: For further information contact Gareth Stevens, New York, New York at 1-800-542-2595.

Contents

Boldface words appear in the glossary.

What Is a Contraction?

Let's go to the zoo to learn about contractions! A contraction is a shorter way of saying two words. An **apostrophe** is used in place of missing letters and spaces.

Let us go to the zoo.

Let's go to the zoo.

Let's is a contraction!

Everyday Contractions

When you make most contractions, you leave out letters.

We're going to meet many animals at the zoo.

We're is a contraction. It comes from the words **we are**.

Loving Life

However, some words change a bit when they become contractions. **Won't** is a short way of saying **will not**.

Some zoo animals **won't** ever live in the wild. These animals are safe and happy in their **habitats** at the zoo!

9

Big Cats

Dangerous animals, such as lions and tigers, live behind fences, walls, or bars at the zoo. **It's** important to follow the rules and stay on your side of the fence.

It's is a contraction made from **it** and **is**!

That's Fishy

Don't bang on the glass! Fish and other **marine** animals that live in tanks might be scared by the noise.

Don't is a contraction of the words **do** and **not**.

Heat It Up!

Some zoo animals, such as parrots, are used to living in warm **temperatures**. You'll sometimes see them in heated rooms or buildings when you visit the zoo.

You'll is a short way of saying you will.

15

Chow Down

Many zoos have an area where visitors can pet or feed animals. However, you **can't** feed all the animals! Zoo animals may be on a special **diet** to keep them healthy.

Can't is a contraction of the words **can** and **not**.

Animals in Danger

Asian elephants are often found in zoos because they are endangered. That means there **aren't** many left in the wild.

Can you figure out what words make up the contraction **aren't**? **Aren't** is a short way of saying **are not**.

Visit the Zoo!

Doesn't the zoo sound fun? You can see animals from all over the world!

Doesn't is a contraction! It's made from the words **does** and **not**.

More Common Contractions

is not   →   isn't

you are   →   you're

I am   →   I'm

should have   →   should've

could not   →   couldn't

he is   →   he's

we will   →   we'll

Glossary

apostrophe: a mark used to take the place of letters in a contraction

diet: the kind or amount of food an animal eats

habitat: the area in which animals live in a zoo. It often looks like their homes in the wild.

marine: having to do with the sea

temperature: how hot or cold something is

For More Information

Books

Cleary, Brian P. *I'm and Won't, They're and Don't: What's a Contraction?* Minneapolis, MN: Millbrook Press, 2010.

Shaskan, Trisha Speed. *If You Were a Contraction.* Mankato, MN: Picture Window Books, 2009.

Websites

Contraction Game
www.learninggamesforkids.com/vocabulary-games/contractions/contraction-game.html
Play games and practice forming contractions.

Match the Contraction
www.oswego.org/ocsd-web/match/dragflip.asp?filename=jwildecontraction2
Practice making contractions in this interactive game.

Index